Make Noise,
Make Merry

Other books by Miriam Chaikin

Light Another Candle
The Story and Meaning of Hanukkah

Joshua in the Promised Land

Shake a Palm Branch
The Story and Meaning of Sukkot

Ask Another Question
The Story and Meaning of Passover

Sound the Shofar
The Story and Meaning of Rosh HaShanah
and Yom Kippur

MIRIAM CHAIKIN

Make Noise, Make Merry

The Story and Meaning of Purim

illustrated by DEMI

CLARION BOOKS

TICKNOR & FIELDS: A HOUGHTON MIFFLIN COMPANY
NEW YORK

In memory of
Edna Barth · Bea Feitler

Acknowledgment
With thanks to Rabbi Lynne Landsberg
for reading the book in manuscript form.

Clarion Books
Ticknor & Fields, a Houghton Mifflin Company
Text copyright © 1983 by Miriam Chaikin
Illustrations copyright © 1983 by Demi
Printed in the United States of America

Library of Congress Cataloging in Publication Data
Chaikin, Miriam.
Make noise, make merry.

Bibliography: p.   Includes index.
Summary: Retells the biblical story of the rescue of
the Persian Jews from Haman's plot to destroy them.
Explains the Purim symbols and tells how the feast is
celebrated.
1. Purim—Juvenile literature.   [1. Purim]
I. Demi, ill.   II. Title.
BM695.P8C46   1983   296.4'36   82-12926
RNF ISBN 0-89919-140-1   PA ISBN 0-89919-424-9
P   10   9   8   7   6   5   4   3

Contents

The Time Before Esther · 1

Esther's Story · 13

How the Holiday Grew · 45

    The Story Is First Told · 45

    The Jewish Year · 46

    The Holiday Takes Shape · 49

    Purim · 53

    Purim Katan · 54

How the Holiday Is Celebrated · 56

    Portions, Gifts, and Foods · 56

    Wine · 59

    The Reading of the Scroll · 60

    Songs · 66

    Purimspiel · 68

    Purim in Captivity · 72

    Adloyada · 74

    Queen Esther · 75

    Righteous Gentiles · 80

Purim Glossary and Pronunciation Guide · 85

Books That Tell About Purim · 87

Index · 89

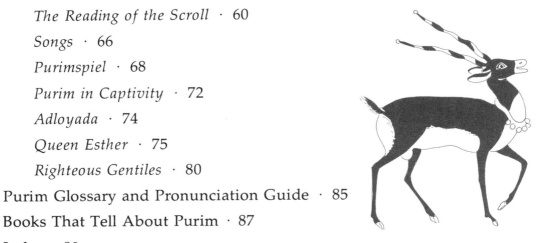

Jerusalem

Babylon

Shushan

Kingdom
of
Ahasweros

The Time Before Esther

The Esther story takes place in ancient Persia (modern Iran) in the fifth century B.C.E. Esther, a young Jewish maiden, shares the Purim story with her uncle, Mordekhai. The land of the Jews was Judah (modern Israel). It lay some nine hundred miles to the west of Persia. Yet the story takes place in Persia. Why is that?

Let us see.

In 598 B.C.E., Nebuchadnezzar, king of Babylonia (modern Iraq), ruled the East. When he conquered Judah, he ordered the Jewish king and all noble families exiled to Babylon, his capital city. The command to his officers in Judah was clear:

Take captive only those in whom there is no blemish but who are well favored, who are wise and educated and who possess a knowledge of science and languages.

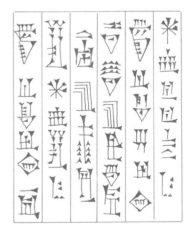

Cuneiform writing
from Babylon

1

As a result of this order, some three thousand Jews were taken captive. Riding camels or walking beside asses loaded with household goods, they made the long trek east to Babylon. (Among them was Daniel, who later found himself in the lion's den. But he does not figure in our story.)

Why did Nebuchadnezzar exile only the noble families? He thought that if he removed the teachers and scholars from Judah, the Jewish nation would, in time, die away. But he was wrong. The Temple in Jerusalem, not the educated class, was the center of Jewish life. The students who had been left behind became teachers. And before long a new generation of teachers and scholars arose in Jerusalem.

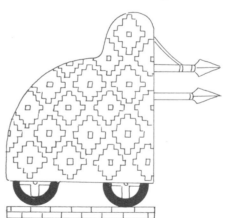

Seeing that this was so, Nebuchadnezzar attacked Jerusalem again. This time he was more thorough. He destroyed the Temple, seized the Temple treasures, and destroyed the city of Je-

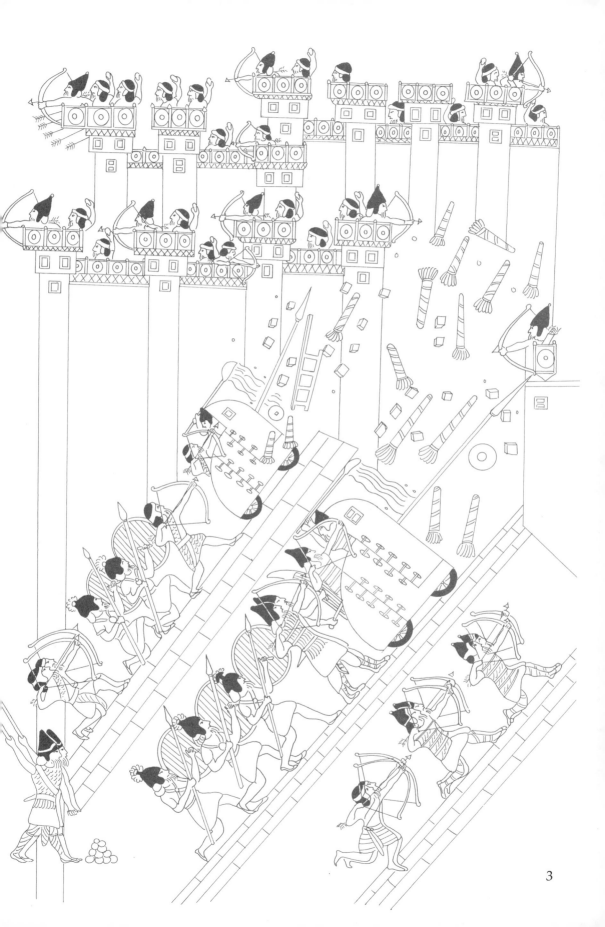

rusalem. And to prevent the Jews from rising again, he exiled the entire population. Only a few vineyard workers and other peasants were left behind. Some exiles went to Egypt, some to Persia. Most went to Babylon, where there was already a large Jewish community.

In Babylon, the exiled Jews grieved for their ruined capital, Jerusalem. But Jeremiah, a prophet of the time, urged them to accept their fate and build new lives for themselves in Babylon. He said:

Seek the peace of the city and pray to God to bless it, for in the peace of the city lies your own peace.

The Jews took his words to heart. They learned Chaldean, the language of Babylon, and settled into the life of the city. Soon, Jewish academies of learning arose throughout the city.

In 539 B.C.E., Cyrus, king of Persia, defeated

Babylon. Now it was the time of Persia to rule the East. This great king encouraged the return of captive peoples to their native lands. He urged the Jews to go back to Jerusalem and rebuild their Temple. He even made them a present of the Temple treasures that Nebuchadnezzar had taken.

In 538 B.C.E., Zerubbabel, the Jewish king, led some 42,000 Jews from Babylon to Judah. Most Jews, however, found it too difficult to uproot themselves and their families, and so they remained in Babylon.

Under Cyrus, power shifted from Babylon to Susa, or Shushan, the capital of Persia. Cyrus' reign was a short one. When he died, Khshayarshan became king. The Jews called him *Ahasweros,* and the Greeks called him *Xerxes.*

The Esther story takes place at this time. Shushan was the king's winter capital. In summer, the heat of the city was unbearable. But in the cooler winter months, Ahasweros ruled from Shushan, which was built on a hill. His palace in the upper part of the city was surrounded by a wall two and a half miles long. Ministers and

other citizens also had their homes inside the walls. Outside, in the lower part of the city, were other homes, the city square, and the marketplace.

The Esther story tells us that Mordekhai sat inside the king's gate. This lets us know that he had a privileged position. He may have been a gatekeeper, a scribe, or a translator — or a combination of all three. We don't know when he arrived in Shushan. We know only that his grandparents were among the noble families exiled from Jerusalem years before, and that he was educated and knew languages.

As the capital of Persia, Shushan was the capital of the East. It was a city of opportunity for educated people like Mordekhai. Most kings and nobles could not read or write. They had to hire scribes to perform the service for them. They also had to hire translators. The kingdom of Persia consisted of more than one hundred provinces. Many different languages were spoken. That presented a problem. The problem was solved by making Aramaic the official language of the empire. Translators were needed to translate government orders from Aramaic into the many languages of the empire.

The Purim story opens in about 485 B.C.E. In ancient days, time was reckoned by the reign of a king. *In the third year of king so-and-so,* a document would say, fixing a time. Later, when scholars tried to translate reigns into calendar years, differences of opinion arose. Ancient dates are therefore inexact.

Ahasweros, when the Esther story opens, is married to Vashti, the granddaughter of Nebuchadnezzar. And at this time, the position of the Jews began to change. Ahasweros' officers in Jerusalem were angry at what Cyrus had done. They did not want to see the Jews returning to Jerusalem and rebuilding a Temple. The Persian officers liked the role of rulers. They wanted to continue in command. But the returning Jews felt differently. They did not see why they should be told by Persian officers what they might and might not do in their own land.

The officers wrote to Ahasweros:

As the king knows, the Jews that Cyrus sent back are rebuilding the Temple. If they are allowed to complete the Temple, they will become strong again and will pay you no taxes or tolls. Nor will they obey your law, but only their own law, given them by their prophet, Moses.

The charge was untrue. Jews paid their taxes. They obeyed the king's law and also their own religious laws. There was no conflict between the two. But talk of loss of revenue made the king nervous. So did the complaints of his officers in Jerusalem. To silence them, he wrote:

I have read and understood your words, and command you to halt the rebuilding of the Temple.

The work was halted. The Jews no longer felt favored, as they had under Cyrus. At this time and in this political atmosphere, the story of Esther came into being.

Now, in those ancient days stories were not written down. Stories were spoken. A storyteller would appear at the marketplace, or wherever people gathered, and tell stories. If a story was about the king, the storyteller did not have to supply details about palace life. He did not have to say where the king lived and how the king lived. The audience already knew that. He had only to lower his voice, or gaze heavenward in exasperation, and the audience would laugh. Storytellers are gone from the scene now. We have books instead. But what palace life was like in ancient times is not well known today.

So in this version of the Esther story details about where the king lives and how he lives have been added. And the conjectures, or guesses, of various scholars have been woven in, along with fictional elements such as dreams. Even so, the essential story, as the Bible tells it, is unaltered and remains intact. It still turns on the same toss of marked stones — square stones of chance called *puru* in ancient Persia and *purim* in ancient Palestine.

Esther's Story

King Ahasweros

After the time of King Solomon, and before Alexander, the Persian king Ahasweros ruled in the East. His lands lay in a perpetual summer, and to escape the heat he ruled now from Babylon, now from the Persian capital of Shushan.

When his astrologers told him the time was right for a war with Greece, Ahasweros went to make war, but without success.

Ahasweros resented defeat. But his ministers flattered and praised him. They reminded him of his power, saying he ruled 127 provinces from Ethiopia to India. And that the governor of each province was a loyal grandee that he himself had chosen. Soon the king's mood lifted.

To celebrate the third year of his reign, Ahas-

weros made a wine banquet for those who governed for him in the provinces. The palace in the upper city of Shushan was decorated with flags. Banners flew from the wall that surrounded the city. The servants set out golden couches in all the courts. And that winter they came to Shushan from far and near, the king's governors with their wives and servants.

The men reclined with the king in the large court. The women reclined with Vashti, the queen, in the garden court. In both courts, slaves went from couch to couch with golden platters and ewers, offering fruit and wine. And for 180 days, that is, six months, or half a year — for that is how long the banquet lasted — grandees and their wives made merry in Shushan.

When the banquet was over, Ahasweros made a small banquet for seven days, for the people of Shushan.

Mordekhai

Now, Mordekhai was a scribe and a well-known Jew in Shushan. He had a seat inside the king's gate. From there, he wrote letters and translated documents for the king, his harem, and others of the palace. He lived with Hadassah, a young niece, whom he had raised from birth. Hadassah was as yet too young for banquets. But on the last night of the banquet, Mordekhai left her

in the care of Hatach, the family servant, and went to make merry with his friends.

When Haman, a minister to the king, entered, Mordekhai looked away. Haman was repellent to him. The man was an Amalekite, a descendant of King Agog, and the Amalekites were a cruel, inhuman race that feared not God. A thousand years before, when Mordekhai's ancestors wandered in the Sinai wilderness, Amalekites fell upon them and slew them.

When the last guests had left, the king reclined yet a while longer with his ministers. They drank wine and spoke of beautiful women. The king boasted that Vashti, the queen, was the most beautiful woman of all. No one denied it. Who would dare? Even so, the king sent Charshena, one of his ministers, to bring Vashti, so that all might gaze upon her beauty.

Charshena returned alone. And he told the king that Vashti was angry, that she resented being summoned at so late an hour, that she refused to come. Ahasweros became enraged.

"You have heard the queen's answer!" he cried, looking at his ministers. "What does one do with such a queen?"

The ministers were just as offended. Queen or commoner, no wife was allowed to disobey her husband.

Mehuman spoke first. "Vashti has wronged not only the king but all the men of Persia," he said. "When the other wives hear what she has

יָפֶן הַמֶּלֶךְ לִרְעוּתָהּ הַטּוֹבָה מִמֶּנָּה: וְנִשְׁמַע
פִּתְגָּם הַמֶּלֶךְ אֲשֶׁר־ יַעֲשֶׂה בְּכָל־מַלְכוּתוֹ כִּי
רַבָּה הִיא וְכָל־הַנָּשִׁים יִתְּנוּ יְקָר לְבַעְלֵיהֶן

done, they will also disobey their husbands, and soon the disease will spread throughout the empire."

"Mehuman speaks the truth," said Haman.

"If it please the king," Mehuman said, "let a law be passed removing Vashti as queen."

It pleased the king. For that had been his own thought. He had no need to utter it now. Later, when he told the secretary what to write in the Royal Book, he would be able to say with truth that the ministers had caused Vashti's removal. But, for now, he sent for a scribe, for the ministers were waiting for him to make a new law. Ahasweros dictated these words: *Every man is a ruler in his own house and must be obeyed.*

A minister advised the king to make the law stronger. The minister saw another danger to the empire. Persian men often married foreign wives. Their children grew up speaking the language of the mother.

The king agreed, and added these words: *All in the house must speak the language that the man speaks.*

The King's Harem

Vashti disappeared. Where she went and how she went, no one knew. The king's Royal Book revealed nothing. The people whispered that Vashti had been beheaded, for so were unwanted wives disposed of at that time.

Soon, the king began to miss Vashti. To turn his anger away from themselves, the ministers advised him to marry again. There were many beautiful maidens in the king's harem. But none pleased him enough to marry. So he ordered the harem keeper to assemble yet other beautiful maidens, so that he might choose a wife from among them.

Each winter, when the king returned to Shushan, the new maidens were brought before him. But he found no wife.

As happens with passing years, Hadassah, Mordekhai's niece, had grown up and become a beautiful young maiden. And when the harem keeper saw her, he chose her for the harem.

Mordekhai spoke with his niece before she left for the palace. "I had a dream in which I saw a little stream become a mighty river," he said. "If you are chosen queen, it will not be just to wear a crown, but for a purpose. In the meantime, reveal not that you are a Jew. The times are not good for our people."

Hadassah lived in the palace harem for a year, for so it was with the harem maidens. The harem keeper favored her and gave her the best room for herself. He gave her maidens to massage her with oil and others to teach her how to use spices and sweet odors. He knew not the name Hadassah as a Jewish name. But, to make her even more pleasing to the king, he changed her name to Esther, a Persian name.

Now, Mordekhai was known in Shushan as a Jew. So that no suspicion might fall on Esther, he remained away from her. But at all times he knew how she was and what she did. For the harem keeper was his friend. And Mordekhai

could ask innocently about the new maiden
without arousing curiosity.

In the seventh year of the king's reign, Ahasweros again went to Greece, trying to make of
it his 128th province. Again he did not succeed.
He returned to Shushan in the eighth month,
the month of Heshvan, and when he saw
Esther, he loved her at once. And in the tenth
month, the month of Tevet, at a great wedding
banquet, he made her his queen.

Esther

The king gave Esther jewels of lapis and seven
maidens to serve her. But Esther was not happy.
She was separated from her people and their
way of life. Also, palace life was lonely. The king
lived in one part of the palace, and she in another. She could not see him whenever she
wished, but only when he sent for her. That was
the law. If she did otherwise, she would risk
death.

When Esther next saw the king, she asked for
permission to bring Hatach, her former servant,
to the palace. The king agreed, and Hatach arrived. Now Esther could keep the dietary laws
of her people without revealing that she was a
Jew. For Hatach prepared her meals. He made
lentil patties for her to eat, and peas and beans.
On the Sabbath, Esther rested. Her maidens so

loved her that they rested along with her, not knowing what it was and why it was.

Now that Esther was queen, she and her uncle could meet often and without risk. For when the queen wanted a letter written or a document translated, she sent for Mordekhai the scribe.

In the twelfth year of Ahasweros' reign, Mordekhai saved the king's life. From Mordekhai's seat inside the king's gate, he overheard Bigtan and Teresh, two gatekeepers from Tarshish, plotting to poison the king's wine. Mordekhai hurried to warn Esther. The queen told the king what she had heard and how she had heard it. And the king sent Haman to investigate. When Haman returned, saying the two men were enemies and had plotted against the king, the king ordered them hanged. The details of the event, where it was and who it was, the king recorded in his Royal Book. And Haman he promoted to prime minister.

Haman

Now, the prime minister was second in importance to the king. And Haman enjoyed seeing the Persians bow to him as he passed. He failed to notice that Mordekhai did not bow down to him. Mordekhai could not bring himself to bow down to an Amalekite. One day, when

Haman went to the palace with one of his ten sons, the son spoke of it.

"Behold," said the son. "The scribe remains standing when you pass."

Haman saw that it was so and became enraged. He vowed to kill Mordekhai. But the thought did not content his anger. So he decided to kill not only the scribe but all the Jews of Shushan. To do that, he needed a lucky date. For no plan could succeed if luck was missing from it.

Haman hastened down to the lower city, to a fortuneteller he knew.

"I have a plan for the good of the empire," he told the man. "Ask the *puru* when I should carry it out."

The fortuneteller took up his marked stones and said,

> *Puru, puru*
> stones of grace,
> on the truth
> turn up your face.

With closed eyes, he added, "This is the first month, the month of Nisan, in the twelfth year of the reign of Ahasweros. Is this the lucky month of the prime minister? If so, show your face." He opened his eyes and tossed the stones.

They fell face down. Each time he threw them, they fell face down. On the twelfth throw, they

fell face up. Adar was the twelfth month of the year.

Haman now needed a lucky day.

The fortuneteller began another round of throwing, and the stones fell face up on the thirteenth throw.

The Law against the Jews

Haman now went to the palace to ask for the king's permission. As he thought about what he would say, his plan grew. Adar was eleven months away. Why kill only the Jews of Shushan? There was time enough to kill all the Jews of Persia.

When the guards outside the throne room told the king that Haman wanted to see him, the king waved his golden scepter toward the court where Haman stood waiting, and the prime minister went in.

Haman bowed before the king. "I have learned of a threat to the kingdom," he said. "There is a certain people scattered throughout the lands. Their laws are different from ours, their ways unlike our own. It is not in the welfare of the king to allow such people to live. If it please the king, let a law be passed that they be destroyed."

Haman knew the king was about to ask the name of the people and how much the destruction would cost. He decided to answer the

money question with such generosity that the king would forget about the people.

"It will cost the king nothing," he said. "I will add ten thousand talents of silver to the king's treasury. That will be enough to pay for the soldiers, and more."

The king removed his ring and placed it on Haman's finger. "The soldiers are yours, the people also. Do with them what seems right to you," Ahasweros said.

Haman rejoiced in his good fortune. He had hoped only to win permission. With the ring he had won the right to make laws. Even so, he hurried through the palace looking for a scribe. For the king was fickle and known to change his mind.

"Write!" Haman said to the scribe, and dictated these words.

To all those who govern for the king:

You are ordered to destroy, slay, and exterminate all Jews, young and old, children as well as women, on the 13th day of Adar, and to plunder their possessions for the royal treasury.

Couriers rode out with translations to the provinces, and a copy was put up in the city square. When Mordekhai and the Jews of Shushan read the law, they tore their robes in mourning, and wept. Their lamentations reached the palace, where the queen heard the cries and sent a maid to find out the cause.

When the maid returned and said that Mordekhai and the Jews were in mourning, Esther's heart fainted. She sent for Hatach and said, "Go at once to my uncle and inquire of him what it is and why it is."

Hatach went and returned, carrying the words of the niece to the uncle and of the uncle to the niece.

Mordekhai said, "Tell the queen to go in to the king and plead with him for the life of her people."

Esther, fearing for her life, answered, "Tell my uncle I advise patience. I have not seen the king for thirty days. He will surely send for me soon. I will speak of it then."

Mordekhai replied, "Think not because you are queen that you will be spared. If you do nothing to save your people, help will come to them from elsewhere. But you and your father's house may perish."

The words stung Esther. She recalled her uncle's prophecy about her wearing a crown. Shamed by her fear and hesitation, she said, "Tell my uncle to assemble the Jews of Shushan. Let them fast for three days. I and my maidens will do the same. Although the law forbids me to go in to the king, I shall do so. And if I perish, I perish."

Mordekhai answered, "But these three days include the first day of Passover. It is forbidden to fast on Passover."

Esther replied, "Uncle, can there be a Passover if there are no Jews?"

The conversation ended. Hatach went no more between uncle and niece. The fast was begun.

Esther's Banquet

On the last night of the fast, Esther had a dream. She saw two moons pushing apart two golden goblets. When she woke and studied the dream, she understood that the two golden goblets stood for the two most important men in Shushan, the king and his prime minister. But the meaning of the two moons eluded her.

To prepare herself for the king, Esther bathed in scented water and put on royal robes. She feared for her life, but she went to the throne room. On the way, the meaning of the two moons came to her. They stood for two days. The dream had told her not to plead with the king today but to wait for tomorrow.

Her heart fainted when the guards stopped her with their spears outside the throne room. But when she looked up, she saw the king beckoning to her with his golden scepter. With trembly knees, Esther went in.

"You risk your life in coming," the king said. "What is your wish? If it is something, name it. If it is someone, name him. Half my kingdom is yours."

The king's affectionate tone revived Esther. The dream had told her to postpone her plea. But she could not stand there in silence. She had come to say something. "If it please the king," she said, "let him come to a wine banquet that I have prepared for him. And let him bring his prime minister," she added. (For was Haman not the second goblet?)

"For this have you risked your life?" asked the king.

"I shall reveal my reasons later," Esther said.

The king sent a slave to bring Haman to the banquet, for the etiquette of the court was to send a slave to escort a royal guest to the palace.

At the banquet, Ahasweros, Esther, and Haman reclined on separate couches in the garden court. Serving maids went from one to the other with wine. It contented Esther to see the king's good mood.

"My queen," said the king, "when shall I hear your wish?"

Esther still knew not the full meaning of her dream. But she let herself be guided by it. "Let the king and his prime minister come again tomorrow night, to a second banquet," she said. "I will speak of it then."

An Unforeseen Event

As Haman left the palace, he saw that Mordekhai did not bow down to him. He let the insult pass. He was full of high spirits at being the only guest at a royal banquet, and hurried home to boast about the evening.

"I was the only guest with the king and queen," he said to his wife and friends. "Tomorrow night I am invited to a second banquet. Only one thing stains my joy. Mordekhai, the Jew who sits inside the gate, refuses to bow down to me."

Answered Zeresh, his wife, "Why poison yourself with hatred? If the king has given you permission to kill an entire people, surely he will allow you to kill one man. Order a gallows built and hang this Mordekhai now. Then you will be able to go merrily into the banquet with the king."

Haman ordered a gallows built and went home to wait for morning. While he slept in a darkened room, all the candles burned in the royal bedroom. But the king tossed and turned. Whether from too much wine or another cause, sleep eluded Ahasweros like a victory in Greece. He sent for his secretary and had the fellow read to him from the Royal Book.

The secretary read about the king's victories,

then about the king's good works. Then he read the list of benefactors to the king. It told of the time Mordekhai foiled the plot of Bigtan and Teresh to poison the king.

"What honor did we bestow upon Mordekhai?" the king asked.

"The book reveals none, O king," the secretary answered.

"Then we must honor him at once," said the king. "Who of my ministers is about? I will consult with him."

The secretary saw Haman arriving in the light of dawn.

"Haman arrives," he said.

"Let him enter," said the king.

Haman bowed before the king. He was about to speak, but the king spoke first.

"What should be done to a man whom the king wishes to honor?" said the king.

Haman was so certain the honor was for himself that he happily let wait his own request. "Such a man should be given a king's robe to wear," he said. "He should sit atop the king's horse, with a crown on his head, and a noble should lead him through the streets."

"Make haste, then," said the king. "You are that noble. Mordekhai, who sits inside the gate, is the man I wish to honor. Take him, and do as you have said."

Burning with shame, Haman led Mordekhai's horse through the streets. "Behold, here is a

man whom the king wishes to honor," he called as he went. Then he hurried home to consult with his wife.

Said Zeresh after listening to him, "You are right to grieve for yourself. Mordekhai's star rises, and yours begins to fall."

Esther Pleads for Her People

They were yet speaking when the king's slave came to escort Haman to the queen's banquet. The slave led Haman to a couch in the queen's court, then took his place with the guards against the wall.

Esther saw how pale was Haman and that he trembled. She now understood full well the wisdom of her dream. In the time that she had waited, the desert sands had shifted. Yesterday Mordekhai was a scribe. Today the king had honored him with a parade. And the prime minister had walked alongside the horse.

"My queen," Ahasweros said. "You have promised to reveal your wish tonight."

Now could Esther speak. She looked to Haman, who sat trembling on the couch. "This man, this Haman, has passed a law calling for my people to be slaughtered," she said. "I ask for my life, and the life of my people."

"Who are your people?" asked the king.

"Mordekhai, whom you honored today, is my uncle. I am a Jew," Esther said.

38

"I knew not," said the king. He turned to Haman. "You spoke of 'a certain people,' but you did not say they were the Jews," he said.

Harbonah, one of the guards, requested permission to speak, and the king gave it.

"O king," said Harbonah. "Haman has built a gallows in his garden on which to hang Mordekhai this night." (How he knew is not known, but that he knew we see.)

The king's wrath boiled over. He went to Haman. "Who made you king, that you plan to take a life?" he said. He ripped the ring from Haman's finger.

"Seize him!" he called to Harbonah and the other guards. "And hang him on the gallows that he has prepared!"

Mordekhai Becomes Prime Minister

Ahasweros gave Mordekhai the ring and made him prime minister. Now was Mordekhai second in importance to the king. The Jews of Persia felt the honor. But their fate was unchanged. Slaughter awaited them. For Haman's edict still stood.

"Mighty king," said Esther to her husband. "My people will be slaughtered on the thirteenth of Adar. Cannot the king revoke Haman's law?"

Ahasweros answered. "Alas," he said. "Not even the king can revoke a Persian law. But let

Mordekhai make a new law. He wears my ring. Let him give the Jews the right to defend themselves. My governors must obey the law. They will help the Jews."

On the twenty-third day of the third month, the month of Sivan, Mordekhai passed a new law. Couriers rode out with translations to the provinces. Mordekhai himself went out to the city square to read aloud the law.

In royal robes of blue and white, with a golden turban on his head, he stood before the Jews of Shushan and read:

To all those who govern for the king:
On the 13th of Adar, grant to the Jews the right to defend themselves against their oppressors and to crush all who come against them.

The Puru Prove Wrong

The months passed — Tammuz, Av, Elul, Tishri, Heshvan, Kislev, Tevet, Shevat. Adar arrived. And on the thirteenth day the massacre that Haman had planned took place, but not as he had imagined. The evildoers rose up with swords. To their surprise, the Jews answered back with swords of their own and smote their attackers.

In the evening, the king came to Esther and said, "In Shushan alone, five hundred men have been slain, including Haman's ten sons."

"I have yet more to ask, O king," said Esther. For she had learned of a new plot against the Jews. The evildoers planned to attack again the following day, when there would be no law of self-defense. Esther spoke of it to the king.

"If it please the king," she said, "let the Jews defend themselves one more day. And hang the bodies of Haman's ten sons in the city square as a warning."

The king ordered the hanging. And Haman's ten sons — Parshandatha, Dalphon, Aspatha, Poratha, Adalia, Aridatha, Parmashta, Arisai, Aridai, and Vaizatha — swung in the city square. When the evildoers saw the sight, many turned back. Three hundred remained to fight, and they were all slain by the Jews.

Thus ended the work of the evildoers in Persia. The Jews lived in peace, and Mordekhai

became powerful in the land. For was it not written in the king's Royal Book that the queen's uncle was great among the Jews, seeking the good of his people and speaking peace to all his seed?

Esther Asks for a Holiday

As the king did, so did the queen. Esther, too, kept a book. All these events were listed therein. How it was and what it was were written for her by Mordekhai. On the last page of her book are these words:

In my name did Mordekhai write to the Jews of Persia, saying, *Let a day be set aside to honor the time our people were saved. Let us celebrate by sending portions to one another and giving gifts to the poor.* The Jews wrote back saying, *Let a holiday be declared, and let it be kept by all generations.*

How the Holiday Grew

The Story Is First Told

The events in Shushan in 474 B.C.E., and Esther's letter to the Jews of Persia, brought about the creation of Purim. But that was not always the name of the holiday. In its early stages it was known as Mordekhai's Day. At first, the holiday was celebrated only by Persian Jews, usually by a telling of the story to a gathering of people.

Jews from Babylon and Judea who were traveling in Persia heard the story there and took it back home with them. The tale of Esther and Mordekhai was a favorite of ancient audiences. Monday and Thursday were market days. Farmers brought their crops to the market, and people came to buy. Storytellers entertained the crowds with the Esther story and others as well.

By 168 B.C.E., Mordekhai's Day was being celebrated in Judea (now Israel) also.

The political events at that time helped popularize the story, too. In 168 B.C.E. the Maccabees were fighting a war for religious freedom. The Shushan story, with its happy ending, gave them hope. For although it had looked like the end for the Jews of Shushan, mysteriously they were saved. The Jews in Judea faced similar dangers. They, too, hoped for a happy outcome. On the 14th of Adar, and perhaps at other times, the leaders told their people who were gathered in the Judean hills about Mordekhai and Esther and the defeat of the evildoers. And the listeners drew faith from it.

The story may have served other purposes as well. It contains repeated references to Hebrew months. As an exciting story, teachers might have found that children were willing to memorize it. The children would learn the Hebrew language by doing so, as well as the months of the Jewish year.

The Jewish Year

The Jewish year has twelve months. Each new month begins on the new moon. Just as the school year begins in September and the calendar year in January, the Jewish year also has two beginnings.

One is on the seventh day of the month of Tishri (falling sometime in September or October). According to Jewish tradition, that day marks the completion of Creation and celebrates the birth of the world. The holiday called Rosh Hashanah, which means New Year, is celebrated on that day. God is declared sovereign. The year that begins in Tishri may be looked upon as a religious year in the life of the individual Jew.

Another year begins in Nisan (in March or April), with the spring festival of Passover. This holiday celebrates the birth of the Hebrew nation. For the Jews left Egypt as slaves and arrived in the Promised Land as a free people. This year may be looked upon as a year in the life of the nation.

The months in the Esther story refer to the Nisan year. Roughly, Jewish months overlap non-Jewish months in this way:

NISAN	March, April (Passover)
IYAR	April, May
SIVAN	May, June
TAMMUZ	June, July
AV	July, August
ELUL	August, September
TISHRI	September, October (Rosh Hashanah)
HESHVAN	October, November
KISLEV	November, December
TEVET	December, January

| SHEVAT | January, February |
| ADAR | February, March (Purim) (And Haman's lucky month, or so he thought) |

The Holiday Takes Shape

The ancient rabbis who ruled on such things were at first opposed to including the Book of Esther in the Bible. They said it contained no mention of God or prayer, and was therefore not sacred. But the story remained a favorite of the people. It was told year after year on the 14th of Adar, for the holiday.

The rabbis of the second century C.E. bowed to the will of the people and included the book of Esther in the Bible.

They also gave form to the holiday. Esther had suggested that portions, or gifts, be exchanged. And the rabbis made the sending of gifts mandatory. It was called *mishloach manot* in Hebrew. The rabbis also defined the activity. The gifts were to be sent by messenger. They were to consist of at least two items — one was a food that was ready to eat and required no cooking, the other, a drink.

Gifts for the poor, *matanot la-evyonim* in Hebrew, was also made mandatory. These were intended for any people in need, Jewish or not. Such gifts were also to consist of a minimum of two items, one a prepared food and the other

49

money. Poor Jews who received money were expected to give charity as well. They were reminded that there are others who are worse off.

Charity was to be given not only to individuals but also to an institution. The Hebrew name for the custom is *mahatzit ha-sheqel*, contributing half a sheqel. In biblical times people gave half a sheqel each year to the Temple. In Israel today the monetary unit is called the sheqel. As a remembrance of those times, Israelis give half a sheqel to a synagogue or charity on Purim. Jews in other lands give half of the established unit of currency — half a dollar, pound sterling, franc, lira, or whatever it may be. Children are not exempt, but must also give half a sheqel, or a similar donation, to charity.

As for the date, two arose. In Shushan, a walled city, the fighting went on for two days. In the rest of Persia, it lasted only for one day. The rabbis therefore decreed that the holiday was to be celebrated on the 14th of Adar in unwalled cities and on the 15th in walled cities. In modern Jerusalem, a walled city, the holiday takes place on the 15th.

A feast, *seudah*, was also declared to be a part of the celebration. Every celebration comes with its feast. But this feast was called for to echo Esther's feast on the occasion of her marriage and also the feast of rejoicing that took place when the Jews were saved.

Some Persian Jews and orthodox Jews of other lands make it a practice to fast the day before the holiday. The fast symbolically echoes Esther's Fast, *Ta'anit Ester* in Hebrew.

The main feature of the celebration was and still is the reading of the story. The rabbis said it was to be read aloud publicly, and that all men and boys must attend the reading. The leader read the story. The audience played its part. Each time Haman's name was mentioned, the audience whispered, *Cursed be Haman.* When Mordekhai's name was mentioned, they said, *Blessed be Mordekhai.*

In the third century C.E. the rabbis ruled that women were also obliged to attend the readings.

Purim

The name Mordekhai's Day fell away, and the holiday began to be called Purim. Perhaps this happened in the third century, when women began to attend the readings. They might have wondered why the holiday should be called Mordekhai's Day when Esther was the main hero of the story. Perhaps *purim* — the Hebrew word for lots — was a compromise between those who wished to keep the old name and those who thought it should be changed to Esther's Day.

However the name came about, scholars are divided about the origin of the name Purim. Some say the word is derived from the Assyrian word *puru,* which means "stone." Perhaps so. In the story, when Haman needs a lucky date for his evil plan, he has stones cast. This would be like taking numbers out of a hat or tossing dice in our own time. Other scholars say the name comes from the Babylonian word *purruru,* which means "destruction." They may also be right. For Haman sets out to destroy the Jews but is himself destroyed instead. Whatever the origin of the word, Purim seems an apt name for a holiday that celebrates events in which chance, or luck, or destiny played so large a part.

Purim Katan

The Purim holiday, which celebrates the rescue of the Jews in ancient Persia, has given birth to a daughter holiday, *Purim Katan*, Little Purim. These are special or personal purims of thanksgiving. A group or individual saved from death or disaster relates the event to a rabbi. The rabbi arranges to have the event written on a scroll, and then reads it aloud to the congregation in the synagogue that week.

Here are some examples of *Purim Katan*.

Persian scabbard from the time of King Ahasweros

What Happened	When	Where
Samuel Ha-Nagid was saved from a death plot against him.	1039	Spain
A Jewish community found relief when its principal oppressor was executed.	1191	Champagne, France
Jews were saved from destruction during Spanish-Algerian wars.	1540	Algiers, Algeria
Jews received permission to lock the ghetto gates from inside rather than from outside, increasing their security.	1607	Verona, Italy
Raphael Meyuhas escaped death at the hands of highwaymen.	1725	Jerusalem

David Brandeis and his family were freed from the accusaion that they had killed non-Jews by poisoning plum jam.	1731	Jungbunzlau, Bohemia
A synagogue escaped destruction by fire.	1741	Ancona, Italy
The false charge that a Jewish physician had poisoned the king was exposed.	1806	Vidin, Bulgaria
Ten Jewish leaders were saved from execution.	1807	Sarajevo, Yugoslavia

The Purim that celebrates the events of the Esther story is sometimes also referred to as Shushan Purim, for the city in which the action took place.

How the Holiday Is Celebrated

Portions, Gifts, and Foods

Purim is the only Jewish holiday celebrating events that took place outside of Israel. It is a minor Jewish holiday, but the merriest, and noisiest, holiday of the year. All customs grow out of the Shushan events. The portions, or gifts, which are exchanged are often delivered by a child or children in costume. With a basket of gifts, the children set out for the house of a friend, neighbor, or relative. In the basket are the two or more items. The drink might be a bottle of wine or fruit juice. The prepared food can range from candy, fresh or dried fruit, nuts, cheeses, and baked goods to stuffed fish or roasted chicken.

Any of these items may be one of the gifts to the poor. The other, money, may be placed in

Purim plate

the charity box at the synagogue. Or it may be given to an individual or group directly, or through existing charities for the needy.

Purim is celebrated by Jews all over the world. No one menu can be said to be typical of the feast, because tastes differ from land to land and family to family. As at any feast, favorite foods are served. As part of the meal, European Jews and their descendants may serve *kreplach*, boiled dumplings filled with chopped meat. Another popular dish is *verenikes*, dumplings that are

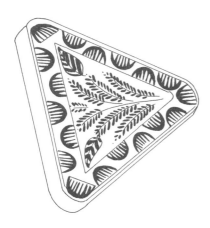

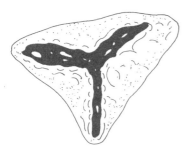

larger than kreplach and filled with chopped meat or liver, mashed potatoes, kasha, or cheese. *Keylitsh*, a very large loaf of braided white bread decorated with raisins, may also be found on the table.

Jews whose ancestors come from Spain or from Arab lands favor *foulares*. This is a shelled hard-boiled egg that has been dropped onto a circle of dough, covered with thin strips of dough, and baked. Children call the pastry Haman's Foot or Haman's Ear. *Nahit* or *bub*, cooked chick peas, is another Purim food. Some say it is eaten on Purim because it was one of the foods Esther ate in the palace, to keep the dietary laws of her people. Others say it is eaten simply because chick peas are tasty when sprinkled with pepper, and they are also inexpensive. Italian Jews serve *orecchi di Amon*, Haman's Ears, a twirled, fried sweet pastry.

Without question, the most visible and the most commonly eaten food on Purim are *hamantashen*, little three-cornered cakes with a filling made of poppy seeds, prunes, dried apricots, or jelly. Originally, the name of this pastry was *mohntashen* in Yiddish, a combination of *mohn* (poppy seeds) and *tashen* (pockets). In time, the *mohn* was replaced by its sound-alike, *haman*, the name of the prime minister who is on everyone's mind on Purim.

Different reasons are given for the three-cornered shape of the pastry. Some say it looks like

At top, at bottom, and on opposite page:
Wooden molds for Purim cakes
from Poland. *Center:* Hamantashen

Haman's foot; others say it is his hat or ear. The real reason may be less colorful. It is a sound baking principle to secure a filled pastry by sealing it at three corners.

Wine

The merrymaking that is so much a part of Purim is a modern re-creation of the Persian wine banquet that was popular in Esther's time. People today do not recline on golden couches to celebrate Purim. They stand or sit in the synagogue, or sit around a table.

The ancient rabbis were at first opposed to the drinking of wine on the holiday. But wine was drunk in spite of their protests. The wine seemed temporarily to ease the pain in times of

trouble, so that after a while the rabbis not only began to accept the drinking, but made it mandatory. They said that it is necessary not only to drink, but to drink *ad de-lo yada*, the Hebrew term for "until you don't know." Until you don't know what? Until you don't know what you're

saying, and you say *Cursed be Mordekhai* and *Blessed be Haman* by mistake!

The Reading of the Scroll

The Scroll of Esther, *Megillat Ester* in Hebrew, is one of five short biblical scrolls. The other four are the Song of Solomon, Ruth, Lamentations, and Ecclesiastes.

The reading of the scroll is the heart of the Purim celebration and its highest point. As a rule, the reading takes place in a synagogue, but it may take place anywhere. If circumstances prevent people from going to a synagogue, they hold a reading wherever they find themselves — at airports, railway stations, hospital rooms, and the like.

In an Orthodox synagogue, the rabbi opens the ceremony with three blessings. All Hebrew blessings begin with the words *Blessed are You, O Lord, our God, King of the universe*. The first blessing is for the procedure, the reading. The second thanks God for the miracles that resulted in the salvation of the ancient Jews. The third thanks God for the gift of life.

Then the Orthodox rabbi, or another reader, sets the scroll out on a table, unrolls it, and begins to read, chanting in Hebrew the story as it has been chanted for centuries. It is not important if the audience does not know Hebrew. They know the story, and do their part.

Ancient audiences used to whisper sedately, *Cursed be Haman*. Audiences today are much more rambunctious. They sit holding something with which to make noise. Most hold a noisemaker, or *gragar* in Hebrew. Others may have two pot covers to beat together, two blocks of wood, or anything else that will make a racket when struck.

The leader reads the scroll, almost singing, for

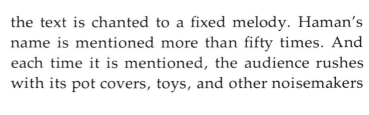

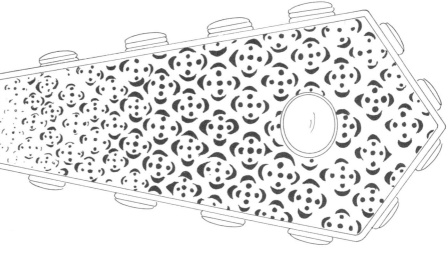

the text is chanted to a fixed melody. Haman's name is mentioned more than fifty times. And each time it is mentioned, the audience rushes with its pot covers, toys, and other noisemakers to fill the room with sound. If they have nothing to make noise with, they hiss, boo, howl, hoot, and stamp their feet — anything to create a ruckus.

What is the object of the noise? To stamp, drown, and blot out Haman's name. The idea comes from the Book of Deuteronomy in the Bible, which says, "You shall blot out the memory of the Amalekites from under the heavens." We are told in the Esther story that Haman was an Amalekite.

The noisemaking of today has replaced the styles of former times. In the Middle Ages, in

Here and on opposite page:
Silver gragar

Spain, people used to clap their hands rhythmically at the mention of Haman's name. Children beat little hammers together. The Jews of Amsterdam in Holland booed and clapped two

stones together. In France, they wrote Haman's name on the stones, so that it might be erased by the clapping. In other places, they wrote Haman's name on the soles of their shoes, to erase it in the stamping.

Another feature of the reading is pronouncing the ten names of the sons of Haman. The reader does this quickly, in one breath, to get it over with. This custom too comes from the Bible. In the Book of Proverbs it says, "Do not rejoice when your enemy fails, do not exult when he is overthrown, lest the Lord be displeased."

The ceremony surrounding the reading of the scroll will vary from country to country and synagogue to synagogue. The Orthodox and Hasidic Jews are emotional. They encourage an outpouring of joy, even of noisemaking. They see the hand of God at work in the story, in the twists and turns of plot that change the fate, or lot, of the Jews. They celebrate the presence of God in all situations.

The Yemenite Jews, though most are orthodox, do not allow noisemakers during the reading of the scroll. They feel the reading ceremony should be more dignified.

The Reform branch of Judaism up to recent times was somewhat reserved in its manner of celebration. Now Reform rabbis display great zest and often wear costumes on Purim. For flavor, they read the opening paragraphs of the Esther story in Hebrew, then continue in English. Nor does the celebration stop there. After the reading, the entire congregation takes part in the program of song, dance, and music that has been arranged. Hilarity is the order of the day.

Every synagogue and Jewish center of any size will have a Purim celebration. As a minimum, the celebration will consist of a reading of the scroll and refreshments afterward — *hamanta-shen* and grape juice or wine. Usually, there will also be a special program for the children. This may feature songs, masquerades, recitations, or

a Purim play performed by the children — or all of these ingredients together.

Songs

Many songs are sung on Purim. "Hag Purim" ("The Purim Holiday") is a popular Hebrew song that young children like to sing.

Hag Purim,	Purim is,
hag Purim,	Purim is,
hag gadol hu la'Yehudim.	a happy Jewish holiday.
Maseykhot, ra'ashanim,	We wear masks and make noise,
z'mirot v'rikudim.	dancing, singing, girls and boys.
Havah naree shaw, rosh-rosh-rosh	Down with Haman, rosh-rosh-rosh
(Repeat twice more)	(Repeat twice more)
ba'ra'ashanim.	twirling noisy gragars.

With older children, "Shoshanat Ya'akov" ("Children of Israel") is a favorite.

Shoshanat Ya'akov,	Children of Israel,
tse'halah v'sameykha	how joyous we were to see
beerotam yakhad	Mordekhai wearing blue
t'khelet Mordekhai.	royal robes of white and blue.
Barukh Mordekhai ha-Yehudi,	Mordekhai blessed be he,

arur Haman asher bi-kesh l'avdi, Cursed may Haman be,
berukha Ester bi'adi, Bless Esther who pleaded for me,
v'gam Harbonah zak-hur la'tov. and remember Harbo-nah too.

"Heint Iz Purim" ("Today Is Purim") is the name of a well-known Yiddish song.

The following is the first verse of a popular English song, "A Wicked, Wicked Man."

Oh, once there was a wicked, wicked man,
the Bible calls him Haman.
He lied and lied about the Jews,
whom he was always blamin'.
Oh, today we'll merry, merry be,
Oh, today we'll merry, merry be,
And *nosh* on *hamantashen*.

Purimspiel

In ancient times there were other traditions at Purim. In the lands of the Middle East, where the holiday started, children used to leave the synagogue after the reading and burn Haman in effigy outside, then jump over the crackling flames.

The Jews of Yemen used to (and still do) light candles in a circle, symbolically burning Haman's ten sons.

In the twelfth century the large Jewish population of Spain celebrated Purim by closing

down businesses, donning costumes — usually those of characters from the Esther story – - and going to visit friends. Children played games in the streets. Jewish students, as a relief from study, made up wine songs, putting comical words to well-known hymns.

In 1492 the Jews were driven out of Spain. They went to live in Germany, southern France, Italy, and other places. There were large Jewish communities all over Europe. By the sixteenth century, Purim was widely celebrated. And an entertainment known as the *Purimspiel,* a Yiddish word that means "Purim play," became a standard. The emphasis was on play, or playfulness.

One or more actors in costume would arrive at the house of a relative or friend and deliver a rhymed monologue about the Esther story. With them, or in their place, were clowns, musicians, or jesters.

Skits, parodies, and masquerades became part of the entertainment. People dressed up as rabbis or political leaders and put on skits making fun of those people. Men dressed as rabbis — they were called "Purim rabbis" — and delivered mock sermons on such subjects as "The Book of the Prophet Bottle." Men dressed as women and women as men. A "Purim King" and "Purim Queen" reigned over the festivities.

The entertainment grew. By the eighteenth

century, full-blown Purim plays were being presented in large auditoriums for an admission price. They might have been current plays, or plays based on biblical stories or on the Esther story itself. The most popular plays were the comic skits in the *Purimspiel* tradition, where heroes and villains were clearly drawn, as they are in a Punch and Judy show.

The *Purimspiel* came to an end in Europe in World War II, when Adolf Hitler and his armies slaughtered the European Jews.

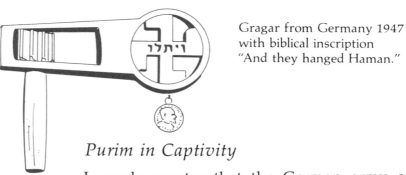

Gragar from Germany 1947 with biblical inscription "And they hanged Haman."

Purim in Captivity

In each country that the German army occupied, they rounded up the Jewish population and sent them to death camps. Some people survived to tell about those times. Sometimes only documents survived.

The Warsaw Diary of Chaim A. Kaplan is such a case. This diary was found in a kerosene can on a farm outside Warsaw after World War II. In it, he tells that Nazis prohibited public worship. Despite the ban, Kaplan and some of his friends managed to gather in secret at the Zionist center on March 13, 1941, for Purim. With Nazis walking about on the streets outside, they could not celebrate in the traditional way. Their Purim feast consisted of bread and butter for each, sweetened coffee, and a shared *hamantash*. Kaplan wrote, "We came sad and left sad, but we had some pleasant moments in between."

Notes from the Warsaw Ghetto by Emmanuel Ringelblum was another such document. He tells of hundreds of Jewish corpses being carried through the streets to be buried in mass graves on Purim. "People hope for a new Purim to celebrate the downfall of the modern Haman, Hitler," he wrote in his diary.

Moshe Prager, in his book *Sparks of Glory*, also speaks of the grim conditions in the early days of the war. The Jews of Vyelun, Poland, to put some cheer into their lives, wanted to celebrate Purim. Although they were not allowed to gather, they knew that the Nazi-appointed Polish guards of the ghetto looked the other way if they received a bribe. The Jews sent the guards some liquor as *shalach manot,* the Hebrew term for a Purim gift. In answer, the guards dragged ten Jews from their homes and hanged them, as a punishment for having hanged the ten sons of Haman.

Jews who managed to escape with their lives joined partisan fighting groups. Lucien Steinberg, a French Jew, writes about the partisans in his book *Not As a Lamb: The Jews against Hitler.* One account involves a Jew fighting in the Ukraine. His name is unknown. His parents, wife, and children had been killed by the Nazis. At the time of the Purim holiday, his commander, Misha Gildenman, ordered him to blow up a trainload of German airmen. The partisan prayed for success, named the mine intended for the Nazis *shaloch moness,* the Yiddish term for a Purim gift, and set out on his mission.

Times of peace can also bring about harsh conditions. In the Soviet Union, people are arrested for political and religious reasons. Shimon Grillius, a "Prisoner of Zion," as Jewish political prisoners were known, could not celebrate Purim in the Soviet labor camp where he was detained. But, wanting to reach out to his people at that time, he wrote a poem of hope whose first lines are

> The wells of exile have no water
> Yet in our hearts are drops of faith.

Adloyada

The largest and most festive celebration of Purim takes place in Tel Aviv, Israel. It is known as *adloyada,* after the phrase of the ancient rabbi telling people to drink until they know not what they are saying. Despite its name, *adloyada* is not a drinking festival but a three-day carnival of fun and entertainment.

The first *adloyada* took place in 1912, in what was then the new city of Tel Aviv. Today, this modern resort city on the Mediterranean Sea is alive for weeks in advance as preparations for the festival get under way. Flags are raised, buildings are decorated, and the names of streets and avenues are changed for the time of the festival to names from the Purim story.

At 6 P.M., on the 14th of Adar, a blast of trumpets announces the start of the holiday. From that moment on, the city crackles with fun and enjoyment. Masses of people watch an elaborate parade with floats and tableaux from the Purim story. Bands play and people dance in the street. Outdoors, there are sporting events and other activities, and indoors, there are concerts, plays, parties, and masquerades. The high point of the festival is the reading of the Scroll of Esther at the city's Great Synagogue. An overflow audience stands outside, under the stars, and listens to the story over a loudspeaker. It is the same story the Maccabees listened to two thousand years ago in Judea.

Queen Esther

Queen Esther has been the subject of controversy for a long time. Scholars, both Jewish and Gentile, have written numerous books and articles about her.

At one end of the argument are those who say that Esther never existed and that the story is fiction. They claim that no Persian king could marry a woman who was not a member of one of the seven noble families. They say Esther's name does not appear among the Persian royal wives. They also find it difficult to believe that the queen would be prohibited by law from visiting her husband unless he sent for her, or that she risked death if she did so.

At the opposite end of the argument are those who say the story is an authentic account of history. They say the list of royal wives is not accurate and that Vashti's name is also missing from it. They say the law that allowed no one to come near the king without permission was called for because relatives and friends were often trying to kill a king. Ahasweros himself was assassinated in his bedroom by his uncle and grandson in 462 B.C.E.

Support for Esther's existence comes also from Josi the Galilean, a rabbi of the second century C.E. He said Esther and Mordekhai had written psalms at the time of the deliverance of the Jews and that these psalms became a standard part of Jewish prayer. Support would appear to come also from Iran, or ancient Persia. Over the centuries and up to our own time, thousands of Jews went each Purim to Hamadan to visit the tombs said to be those of Esther and Mordekhai.

In between these two ends of the argument is a middle position. It says that if Esther did exist, she was not queen, but a maiden in the harem.

The debate continues to this day.

Whether there was a Queen Esther in the fifth century B.C.E. or not, her story exists and is still important today. It has been recited annually for more than two thousand years. Esther, and the things that took place in Shushan, have been a source of inspiration for people in times of trouble. Through the ages artists have also been inspired by the events. The Diaspora Museum in Tel Aviv contains a wall from a synagogue in Syria from 245 C.E. The wall is covered with colored frescoes showing scenes from the Book of Esther.

Christian missionaries working in China in the 1800s found a Book of Esther illustrated in the Chinese style. The drawings were made by a Jewish Chinese artist from Kaifeng, a province of Honan. Jews from Persia had settled there in the 1100s, at the invitation of the emperor.

Chinese Jews at worship

Such great world artists as Rubens, Rembrandt, Botticelli, and Tintoretto have painted scenes from the Esther story. Countless plays have been written about Esther. Handel's oratorio *Esther* is widely performed. Other composers have written music for the story, and designers and artists continually fashion new scrolls and *gragars*.

פַּרְשַׁנְדָּתָא

דַּלְפוֹן וְאֵת

אַסְפָּתָא וְאֵת

פּוֹרָתָא וְאֵת

אֲדַלְיָא וְאֵת

אֲרִידָתָא וְאֵת

פַּרְמַשְׁתָּא וְאֵת

אֲרִיסַי וְאֵת

אֲרִדַי וְאֵת

וַיְזָתָא וְאֵת

עֲשֶׂרֶת

79

Design on
the opening
of a scroll

Esther lives on also in her Hebrew name. Hadassah, the charitable Woman's Zionist Organization founded in 1912 on Purim by Henrietta Szold, took its name from the queen.

Righteous Gentiles

A concept exists among Jews that is said to have its origin in Harbonah's part in the Purim story. Righteous Gentiles, in Hebrew *chasiday umot* ("the righteous of the nations"), are men and women of other faiths who have risked their lives to save Jews in times of trouble.

Yad va'Shem is a Hebrew term that means "Memorial and Record." It is the name of a memorial park on Remembrance Hill in Jerusalem. The buildings, monuments, and gardens of the park honor the heroes, martyrs, and dead of the Holocaust that took place during World War II, in which six million Jews were killed.

A lovely tree-lined walk called the Avenue of Righteous Gentiles is part of the park. It honors the many non-Jews who helped save Jewish lives during the war. Each tree is named for an individual. The individual, or a representative, came to Jerusalem to plant the tree. Some of the better-known Righteous Gentiles are:

• Christian X, King of Denmark, who protected the Jews of Denmark during World War II

• Raoul Wallenberg, a Swedish diplomat who bravely helped many Jews during World War II. (He disappeared in Russia, and the Russians say he died. Others say he is still alive, in a Soviet labor camp. The search for Wallenberg continues, along with the controversy.)

• Corrie ten Boom of Holland, a famous woman underground fighter during the German occupation of her country

• Victor Kugler, in whose home in Amsterdam, Holland, Anne Frank and her family hid during the German occupation

Where does Harbonah come in? In the Esther story, this palace guard tells the king that Haman has prepared a gallows on which to hang Mordekhai. The king, thinking Haman has gone too far by planning to kill Mordekhai without permission, orders Haman hanged. Harbonah's presence — his being in the right place at the right time — is regarded as mysterious and providential. Mysteriously, he knew about what Haman intended to do with the gallows he had built. Mysteriously, he was in the garden court when Esther spoke. Had he not intervened, the king might have been content only to imprison Haman, freeing him to do his mischief at a later time.

According to tradition, then, Harbonah is regarded as having saved Jewish lives, and he is looked upon as the first Righteous Gentile.

The popularity of the holiday of Purim grows each year. Even the *purimspiel* is making a comeback, not only in Europe, but all over the world. This is not to be wondered at, for who does not enjoy an entertainment? The comic plays and skits in the *purimspiel* tradition are fun and a source of pleasure for the entire family.

People like to be allowed to make noise. They also like to make merry. And each year more Jews go to a synagogue, temple, Jewish center, or private home to hear the Esther story read. It

is a link with their ancestors of two thousand years ago, who also listened to the same story being read aloud.

And the people of today like the story for the same reasons as the Maccabees did in 165 B.C.E: It has a happy ending. Good is rewarded and evil is punished. Although things looked hopeless for the Jews of Shushan, "help came to them from elsewhere" to rescue them.

The
End

Purim Glossary

Ad de-lo yada (ad-DELL-lo-ya-DAH) "Until you don't know"

Adloyada (ad-LO yah-DAH) The three-day Purim carnival in Tel Aviv

Ahasweros (ah-hash-WEAR-us) Persian king and Esther's husband

B.C.E. Before the Common Era, which is the way Jews reckon time before Christ, or B.C.

C.E. Common Era

Chasiday umot (hah-si-DAY u-MOTE) Righteous Gentiles

Gragar (GREG-er) Rattle or other noisemaker

Hamantashen (HAH-men-TOSH-in) Three-cornered, filled pastries

Mahatzit ha-sheqel (ma-ha-TSITT ha-SHECK-ul) Contributing the sheqel

Matanot la-evyonim (ma-ta-NOTE la ev-yo-NIM) Gifts for the poor

Megillat Ester (meh-GE-latt es-TAIR) The Scroll of Esther

Misloach manot (mish-lo-AK mah-NOTE) Sending gifts

Nosh (NOSH) a snack

Purim (POOR-im) The Jewish holiday that celebrates the rescue of the Persian Jews from Haman's plot to destroy them

Purim Katan (POOR-im ka-TAHN) A special Purim

Purimspiel (POOR-in-shpeel) A comic entertainment

Purimspieler (POOR-in-SHPEEL-er) A Purim actor

Puru (POO-roo) Assyrian word for "stone" or "lot"

Purruru (POOR-roo-roo) Babylonian word meaning "destruction"

Seudah (seh-u-DAH) Feast

Shalach manot (sha-LOCK mah-NOTE) A Purim gift (Hebrew)

Shalach moness (sha-LUCK MUN-ess) A Purim gift (Yiddish)

Ta'anit Ester (ta-ah-NEAT es-TAIR) Esther's fast

Yad va'Shem (YOD va-SHEM) Memorial and record

Books That Tell About Purim

The Holy Scriptures. Philadelphia, Pa.: The Jewish Publication Society of America, 1955. *Esther,* page 1114, is the biblical account on which all versions of the Purim story are based.

Goodman, Philip. *The Purim Anthology.* Philadelphia, Pa.: The Jewish Publication Society of America, 1949. Stories, customs, poems, activities, and various writings about and relating to the holiday. For ages eleven and up.

Greenfeld, Howard. *Purim.* New York: Holt, Rinehart & Winston, 1982. A brief, stately retelling of the Purim story and a companion to other Jewish holiday books, all illustrated by Elaine Grove and designed by Bea Feitler. For ages ten and up.

Scharfstein, Sol, editor. *Megillat Esther.* New York: KTAV Publishing House, Inc., 1975. The Esther story in scroll form. For all ages.

Suhl, Yuri. *The Purim Goat.* New York: Four Winds Press, 1980. Yossele, a poor Jewish boy, teaches his goat to dance, so it will not be sold. Pictures throughout by Kaethe Zemach.

Weil, Lisl. *Esther.* New York: Atheneum, 1980. A retelling of the Esther story for young children in an appealing picture book format.

Zwerin, Raymond A. and Marcus, Audrey Friedman. *A Purim Album.* New York: Union of American Hebrew Congregations, 1981. The Esther story in the format of a photo album for very young children. Full-color illustrations by Marlene Lobell Ruthen.

Index

Adloyada (Purim carnival in Tel Aviv), 74–75

Ahasweros, King, 5, 8, 13, 16, 23–24, 27–28, 31–32, 33–40, 41, 77; banquet of, 13–14; laws of, 18; marriage to Esther, 21

Amalekites, 16, 24, 62

Aramaic language, 7

Babylon, 1, 4–5, 13

Bible: Book of Esther included in, 49; short scrolls of, 60

Bigtan, 23–24, 34

Chaldean language, 4

Charshena, 16

Cyrus, 4–5, 8, 10

Esther, 1, 5, 7, 10, 21–23, 24, 29–32, 39, 41, 49, 52, 53, 82; did she really exist?, 75–80; her banquets for the king, 32; her dream, 31–32, 36; marriage to Ahasweros, 21; new holiday proclaimed by, 43; revealed as a Jew, 36; *see also* Hadassah

Esther (oratorio by Handel), 78–80

Esther, story of, in art, 78

Esther, telling story of, 45–46

Exiles, Jewish, 1–5

Fortunetelling, 25–27

Gragars (noisemakers), 61, 66, 80

Hadassah, 14, 19–20, 80; *see also* Esther

Haman, 16, 18, 24–29, 32–33, 34–39, 49, 52, 53, 58–59, 61–63, 82

Harbonah, 39, 80, 82

Hatach, 16, 21, 30, 31

Iran, 1, 77

Iraq, 1

Israel, 1

Jeremiah, 4

Jerusalem, 2, 4, 5, 8, 51; Temple in, 2, 5, 8; *Yad va'Shem* ("Memorial and Record"), 81

Jewish exiles to Babylon, 1–5

Jewish year, 46–49; months of, 48–49

Jews: in China, 78; declare new holiday, 43; defend themselves, 41; Esther's story inspiration to freedom, 46; European, 57, 70; exiles from Judah, 1–5; fear and mourning of, 29–31; in France, 63; in Holland, 63; honored through Mordekhai, 39; Italian, 58; of Middle East, 68; new law to protect, 39–40; plot to kill those in Persia, 25–29; of Spain, 58, 62–63, 68–70;

Jews (*continued*)
worsening treatment of, 8–10; of Yemen, 64, 68
Judah, land of, 1
Judea, land of, 46, 75

Maccabees, 46, 75, 84
Mehuman, 16–18
Mordekhai, 1, 7, 14–16, 19, 20–21, 23–25, 29–31, 32, 33, 34, 41–42, 43, 52, 77–78, 82; honors for, 34–35; raised to prime minister, 39–40
Mordekhai's Day, 45, 53

Nebuchadnezzar, 1, 2–4, 5, 8
Noisemakers, 61
Not As a Lamb: The Jews against Hitler, 74
Notes from the Warsaw Ghetto, 73

Persia, 1, 4–5, 7, 51, 77
Purim (holiday), 43, 44, 45, 49; adoption of name for, 53–54; charity for, 51, 56; date of, 51; foods for, 56, 57–59; form of the holiday, 49–53; gifts for, 49–50, 56; how celebrated, 56–66; making merry, 64–66, 68–72, 74–75, 82–84; noise-making, 61–64, 82; Purim Katan, 54–55; *Purimspiel*, 70–72, 82; reading of Scroll of Esther, 60–64, 75, 84; Shushan Purim, 55; songs of, 66–68; wine for, 59–60
Purim in modern captivity, 72–74; accounts of, 72–74

Purim Katan (Little Purim), 54–55; examples of, 54–55
Purimspiel, 70–72, 82
Puru (purim) stones, 11, 25–27, 53

Righteous Gentiles, 80–82
Royal Book of Ahasweros, 18, 24, 33–34, 42

Scribes and translators, 7, 14, 23, 28–29
Scroll of Esther (*Megillat Ester*), 60; reading of, 61–64, 75, 84
Shushan (Susa), 5–7, 13, 14, 45, 46, 51, 56, 78
Shushan Purim, 55
Sparks of Glory, 73
Storytelling, 10–11, 45

Tel Aviv: *adloyada* in, 74–75; Diaspora Museum in, 78
Temple in Jerusalem, 2, 5, 8
Teresh, 24, 34

Vashti, 8, 14, 16, 18–19, 77

Warsaw Diary of Chaim A. Kaplan, The, 72–73
Woman's Zionist Organization (Hadassah), 80

Xerxes, 5

Yad va'Shem ("Memorial and Record"), Jerusalem, 81

Zeresh, 33, 36